A Domestic Lookbook

A Domestic Lookbook

JoAnne McFarland

GRID BOOKS · BOSTON

GRID BOOKS
grid-books.org

Cover: The Ideal Temperature Dress, 2023

Dress images included in *A Domestic Lookbook* are part of an ongoing collage series begun by the author in 1997.
Botanical renderings used throughout come from
An Illustrated Catalog of American Fruits & Nuts, The US Department of Agriculture Pomological Watercolor Collection, atelier éditions.
In order of appearance:

The Half Moon Dress
The Fast Forward Dress
The Great Expectations Dress
The Storyteller Dress
The Dainty Damsel Dress
The Terms of Endearment Dress
The Sixth Sense Dress
The Floating Island Dress
The Two Pugs Dress
The Double Dog Dress
The Lemon Drop Dress
The Guest of Honor Dress
The Black Duchess Dress

Artworks in the section *un–Ruining* are
part of the author's series of Still–ed Life oil paintings
that memorialize Black Americans who
have died violently in the United States.

ISBN 978-1-946830-21-0
First Edition

For Stephen and Lissie

Trigger Warning

A call and response with excerpts from *A Domestic Cook Book,* self-published in 1866 by Malinda Russell, the first known cookbook published by a Black woman in the United States.

Malinda Vaughn, Fashionable Laundress, would respectfully inform the ladies and Gentlemen of Abingdon, that she is prepared to wash and iron every description of clothing in the neatest and most satisfactory manner. Every article washed by her, she guarantees shall pass unscathed through the severest ordeal of inspection, without the remotest danger of condemnation.

Unscathed through the severest ordeal

You wake up breathing
test the power of your hips to hold you upright
Isn't that what makes us human?
Homo erectus
Look at all you can survey, now that you've picked yourself up
off the ground
(that boy is no longer moving
or that woman who was on her way to church)
Some mornings you stumble towards the bathroom in such
agony you wonder how you can possibly go on twenty more years
That's what they predict for someone of your age
Everything has become the fusillade that might stop you
from reaching your *full potential*
Isn't that why we're here?
You're wasting time asking yourself these
questions
Search through the pile for the blue jacket
you bought last week
Don't worry
if it stinks
buried, as it's been, for three whole hours underneath the others

Hearing that Michigan was the Garden of the West, I resolved to make that my home, at least for the present, until peace is restored, when I think of returning to Greenville, Tennessee, to try and recover at least part of my property. This is one reason why I publish my Cook Book, hoping to receive enough from the sale of it to enable me to return home.

When I think

Back in the day

Whites Only

slowed the beat down
like smoke does bees
bees that are dying
Soon there won't be honey
Who will call me *Honey* now that
you are dead?
You told me once
how your mother pretended to be white
to buy you milk
She shook as she entered the General Store
your father and sister left
behind in the Ford too
dark to pass

Being compelled to leave the South on account of my Union principles, in the time of the Rebellion, and having been robbed of all my hard-earned wages which I had saved; and as I am now advanced in years, with no other means of support than my own labor; I have put out this book with the intention of benefiting the public as well as myself.

With no other means

In order for a border to be breached
we must first agree that there's a border
between here and there
you and me
agree that heaven is mine and hell is yours
This territory, this field, air, bird, sky—
these are all mine
In order for my flesh to be breached
we must agree that, by some magic, your body ends
and with it the threat of my violation
For your body to be worth reaching
I may need to, at long last, learn how to swim
Swimming may feel like flying
as the border between me
and your old New World collapses
As salt water bathes my throat
I may come to love both you
and death

Salt Rising Bread

To a half pint warm water, a pinch of salt; stir to a thick batter and keep warm until it rises. To one pint of this rising add three pints warm water, a little salt, and a small piece of lard. Knead the dough until smooth, make into rolls, keep warm until it rises; bake quick, but do not scorch.

To this rising add

the killers
My mother pointed them all out—
that one, and him and him and him
Yes, you may become a target—
See her and her and her?
Wreck yourself with beauty
steal it hoard it draw
It will be how you can bear to leave this
house

Queen's Party Cake

One quart sour cream, six lbs sugar, six lbs butter, five lbs raisins, five lbs currants, one and one-half lbs figs, one ounce cloves, one ounce cinnamon, one and one-half nutmeg, extract of lemon or vanilla, whites of eighteen eggs, yelks of ten eggs, one teaspoonful soda, two teaspoonfuls cream tartar, flour to stir quite stiff.

Whites of

their eyes are not visible in these photos
Were it not for all the blood, this poem
could travel back in time
and find the other missing
colors when the first photographs were taken
Invention, like destruction, requires rage
It is not optional
It's just a matter of direction
Both capture the gore these hostages
produced while not debating the proper
subject
matter for
art

Cold Iceing

One lb pulverized sugar, break in the whites of five eggs on the sugar, beating with a silver spoon or wooden paddle; pound a lemon and squeeze in the juice.

Pulverize beat pound

This emissary appears to be alone
He is a *lone*
wolf
no family no history
Loaded down, he arrives
Later
he will be described as a *loner*
a mist among the living
He will be called *troubled*
and *if onlys* will be cast upon
the graves

Nameless Cake

One teacup butter, one do. sugar, five eggs, one cup milk, two cups flour.

Nameless

I disappeared into his gaze
My mother tried to get rid of me
I just wanted him to be quiet
I clamped him shut in my head
He was too much
I couldn't see
He almost disappeared
My mother says she tried
I was named after my father
I was willing to pray
From the beginning I adored them
He was looking for a boy
He tried to get rid of me
I was willing to know his name
From the very beginning I adored her
I just wanted it to be quiet
Why couldn't we fall asleep?
I clamped down on my tongue
Why couldn't he be a girl?
My father had a girl's name
that's the name I won

(Remarks.—As a great many ladies have wished to know how I have such good success in making my cakes so light, I will say, I first heat the oven hot enough for cooking, set in the cake, and open the door; for a common sized cake leave the door open for about fifteen minutes, and for a large one, about twenty minutes. When the cake begins to raise, close the door.)

Open the door

The day breaks in two
He breaks into the day
We huddle in a daze
Caked with blood eventually we will run
Days built from light
scatter
With one eye I look through
shadow

Burns

After applying sweet oil, scrape the inside of a raw potato, lay it on the burn. In a short time put on fresh potato; repeat it quite often; it draws out the fire and gives immediate relief.

Field & Stream

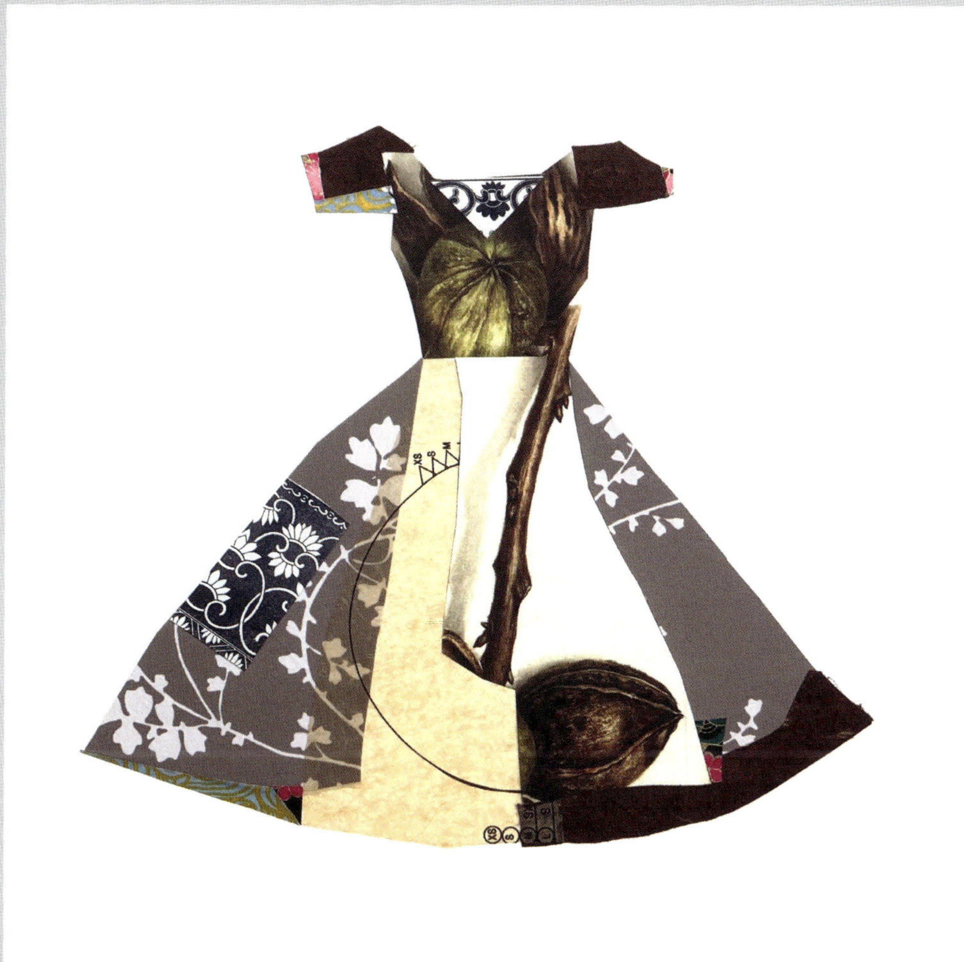

I

Awake at night—

the sound of the past

cracking in the cold

C

E

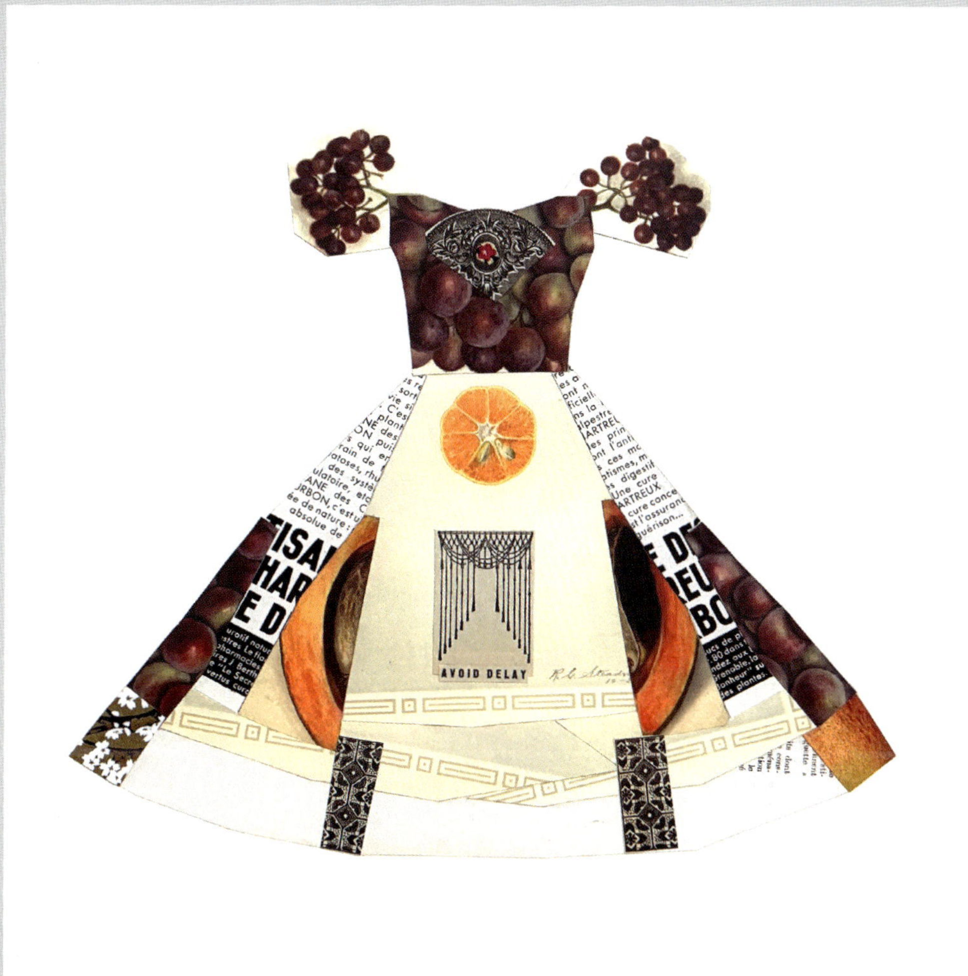
AVOID DELAY

H

O

Weathered bones

on my mind

a tongue-pierced
melon

N

E

Y

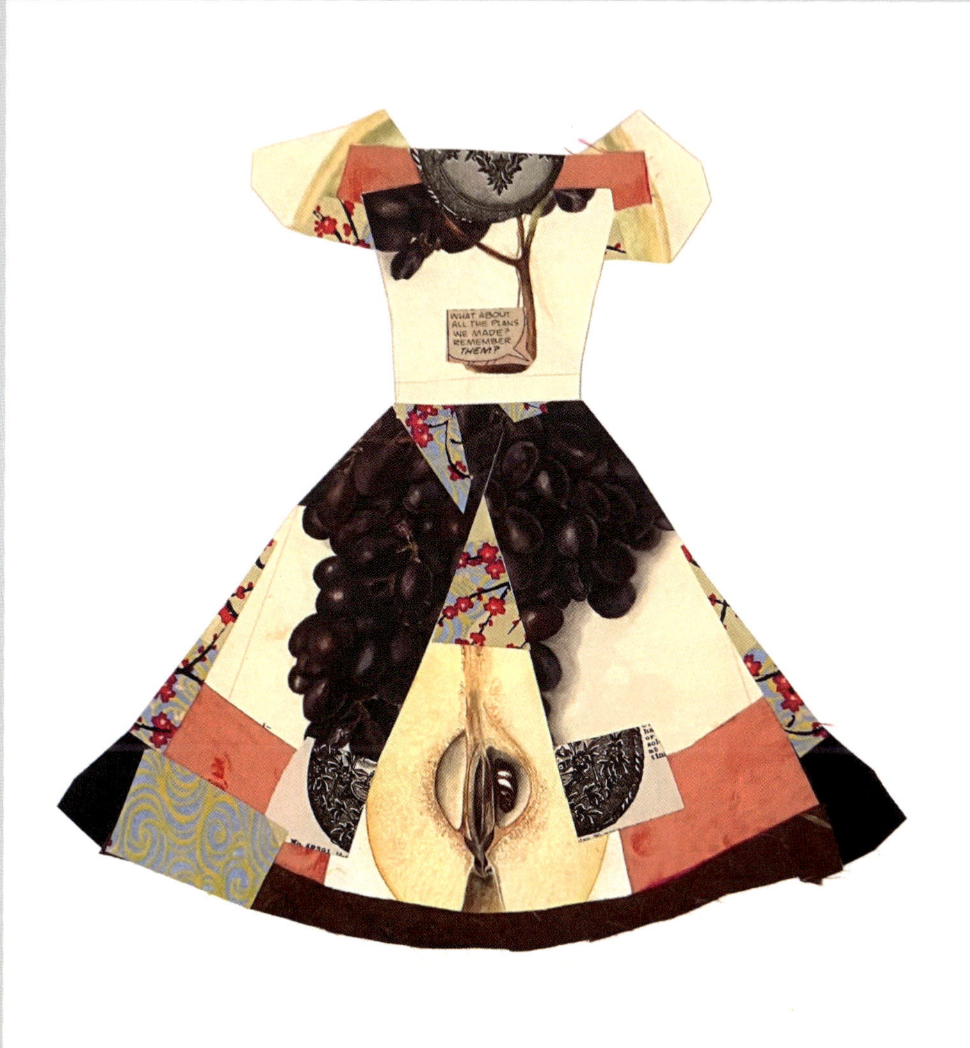
WHAT ABOUT ALL THE PLANS WE MADE? REMEMBER THEM?

V

E

N

I don't know

which enemy it comes from

that fragrance

O

M

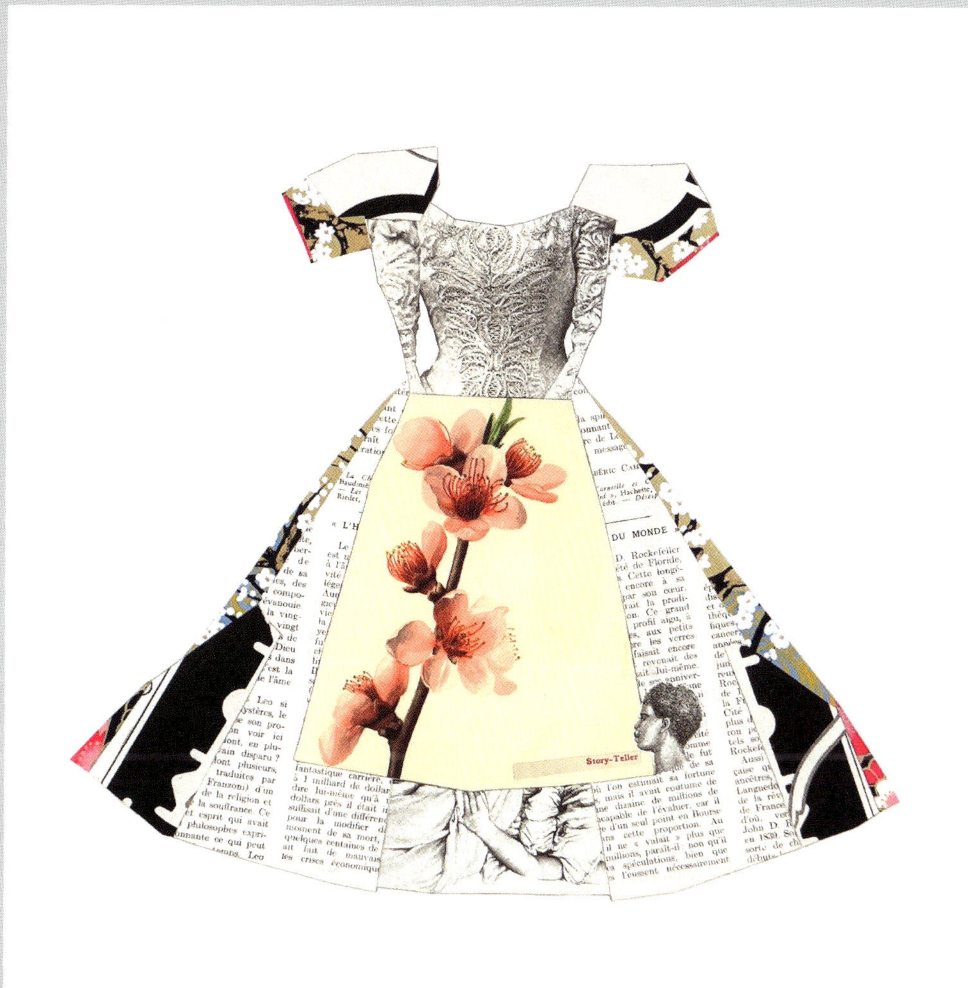
DU MONDE
Story-Teller

S

E

A spooked lover

he sang himself

utterly away

M N

E

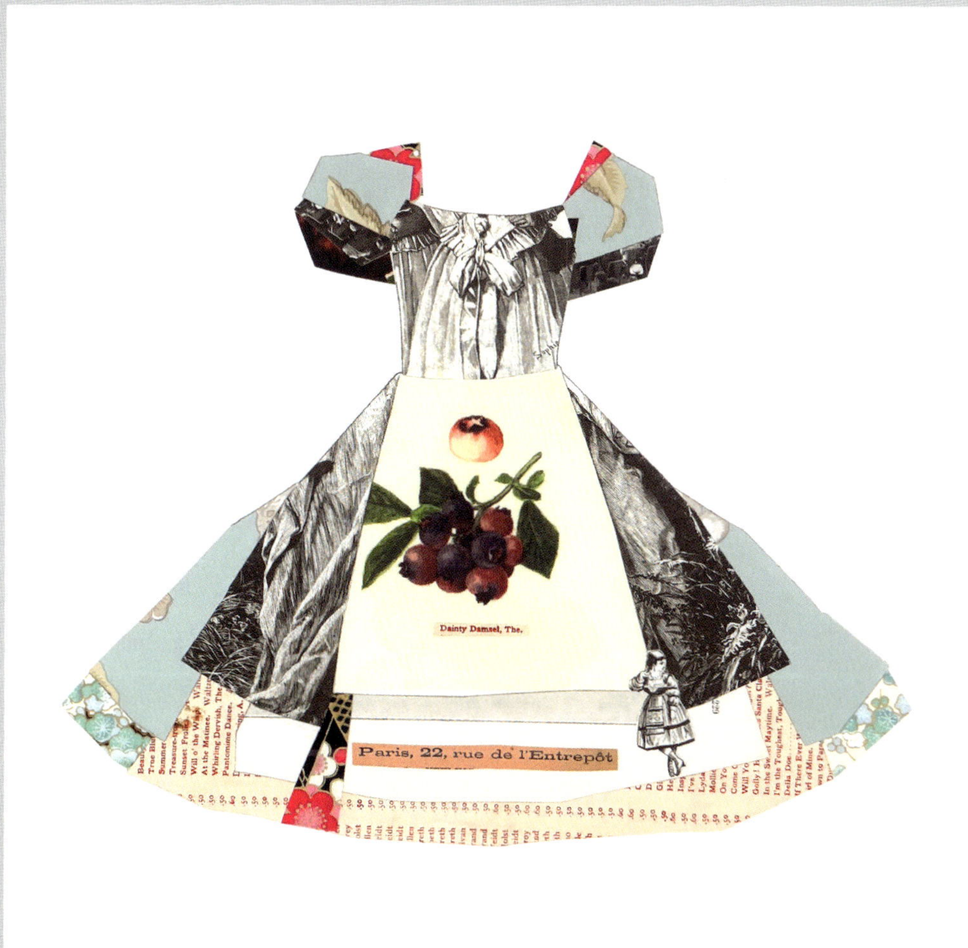
Dainty Damsel, The.
Paris, 22, rue de l'Entrepôt

S

W

Heat waves shimmering

one or two vials

above the bed

T

E

A

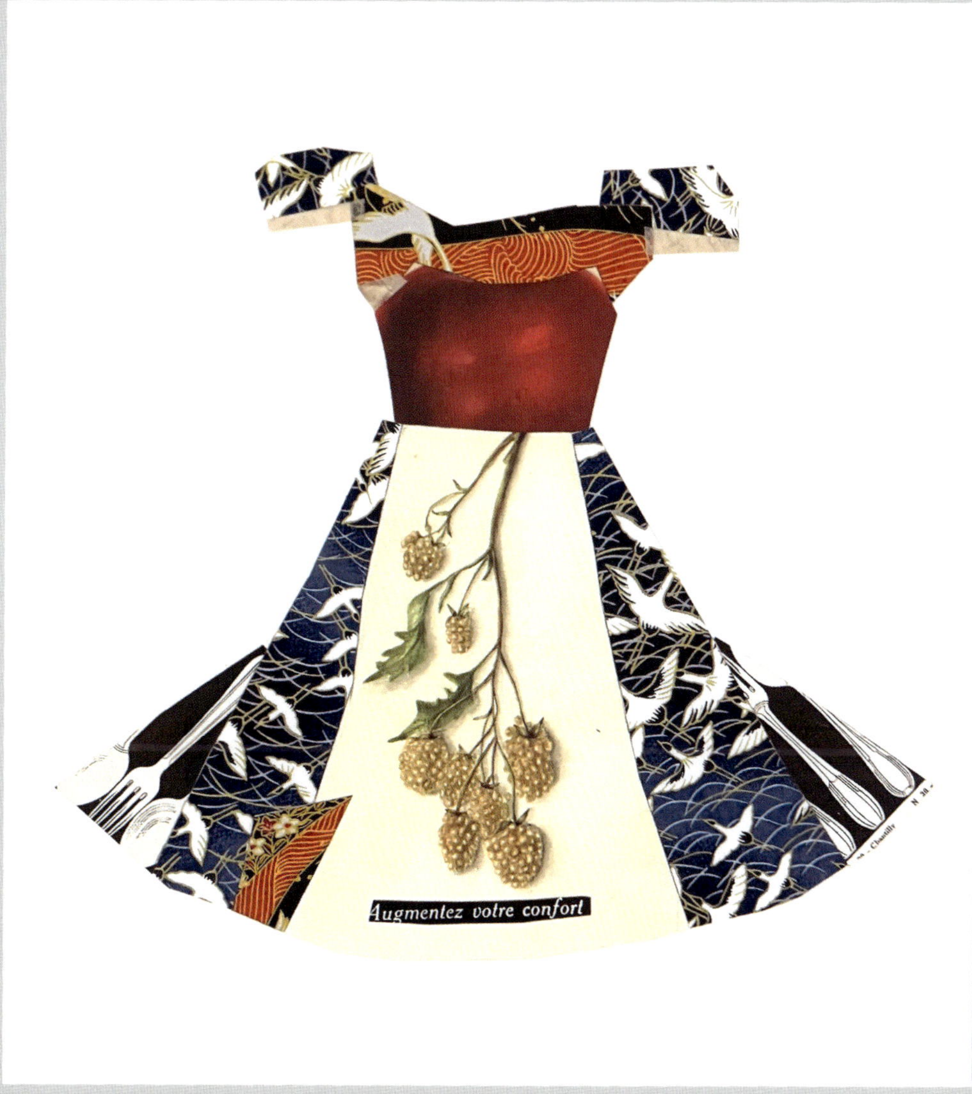
Augmentez votre confort

R

U

S

Monarch butterflies

flit across

rumpled sheets

T

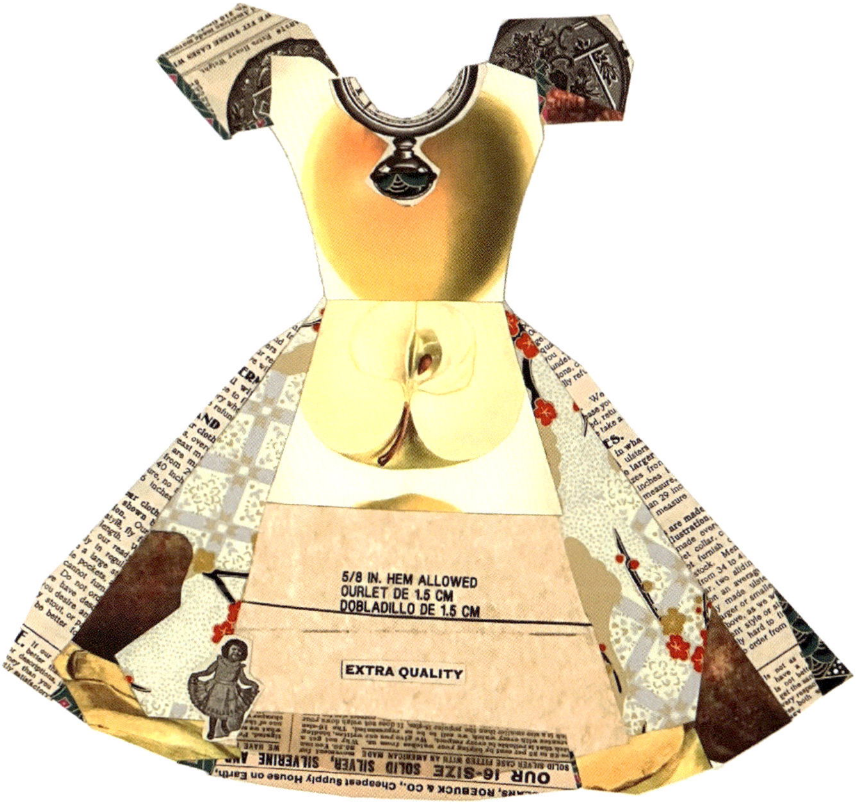
5/8 IN. HEM ALLOWED
OURLET DE 1.5 CM
DOBLADILLO DE 1.5 CM
EXTRA QUALITY

S

A

L

Old scores

I

a curse leaps—

dark sound

A

V

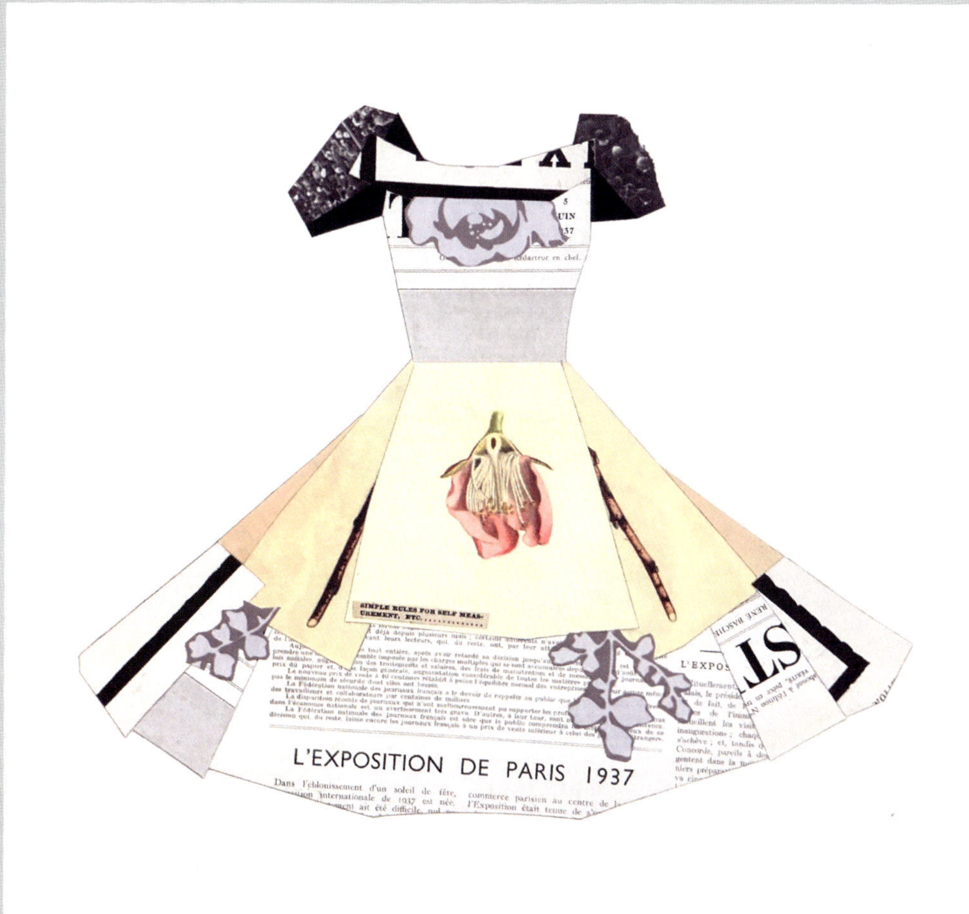
SIMPLE RULES FOR SELF MEAS-
UREMENT, ETC.
L'EXPOSITION DE PARIS 1937

A

S

He lied three times

the kookaburra

then silence

H

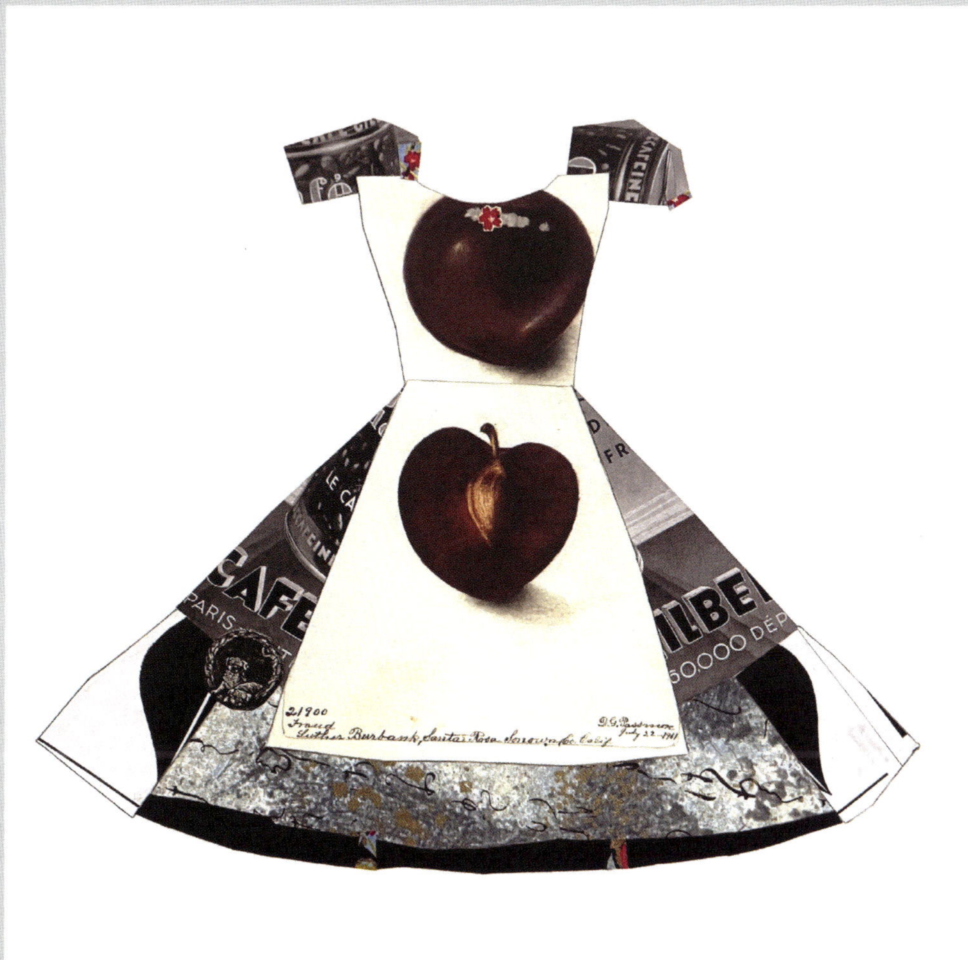
CAFE
PARIS
50,000 DÉP
21900
Luther Burbank, Santa Rosa, Sonoma Co. Calif
D.G. Passmore

T

A watch spattered

with droppings

of chow fun

E

A

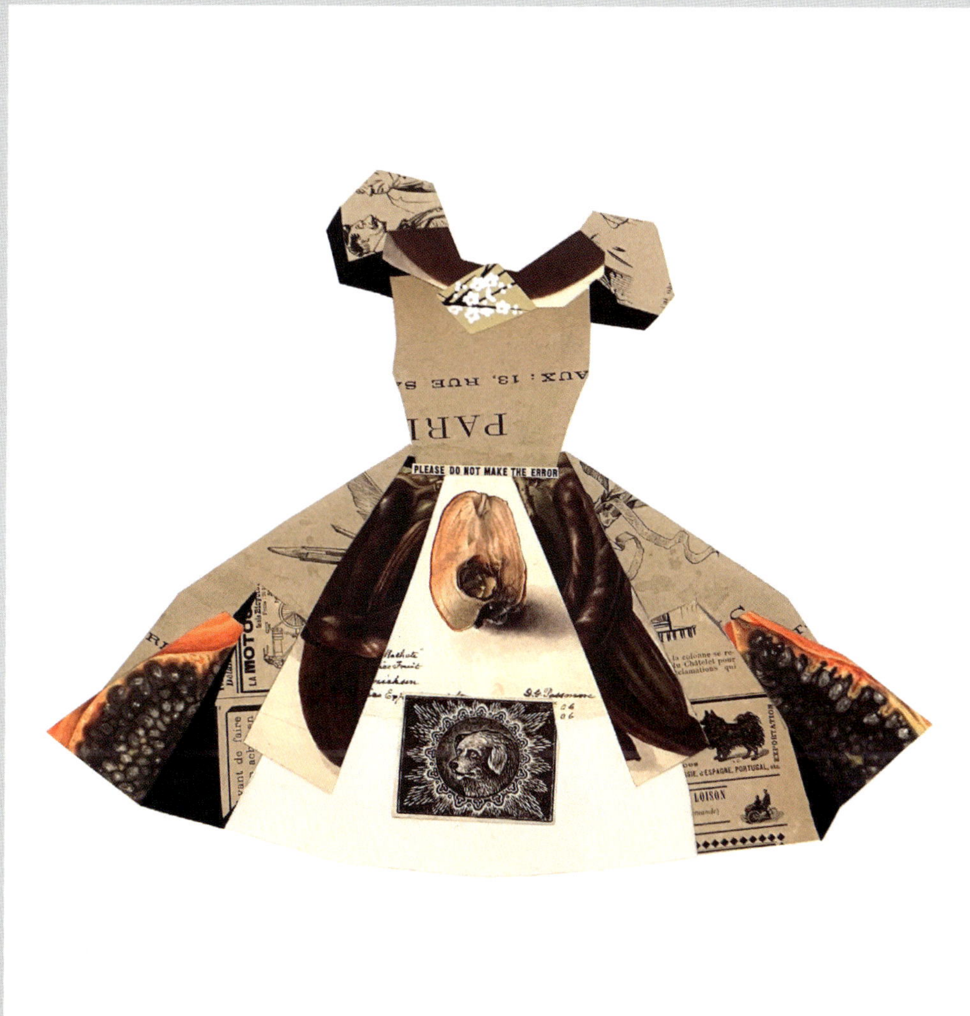
PARI
PLEASE DO NOT MAKE THE ERROR
EXPORTATION
LOISON

S A G

O

Petals scattering—

the kisses I thirst for

far off in the mist

L

I

N E

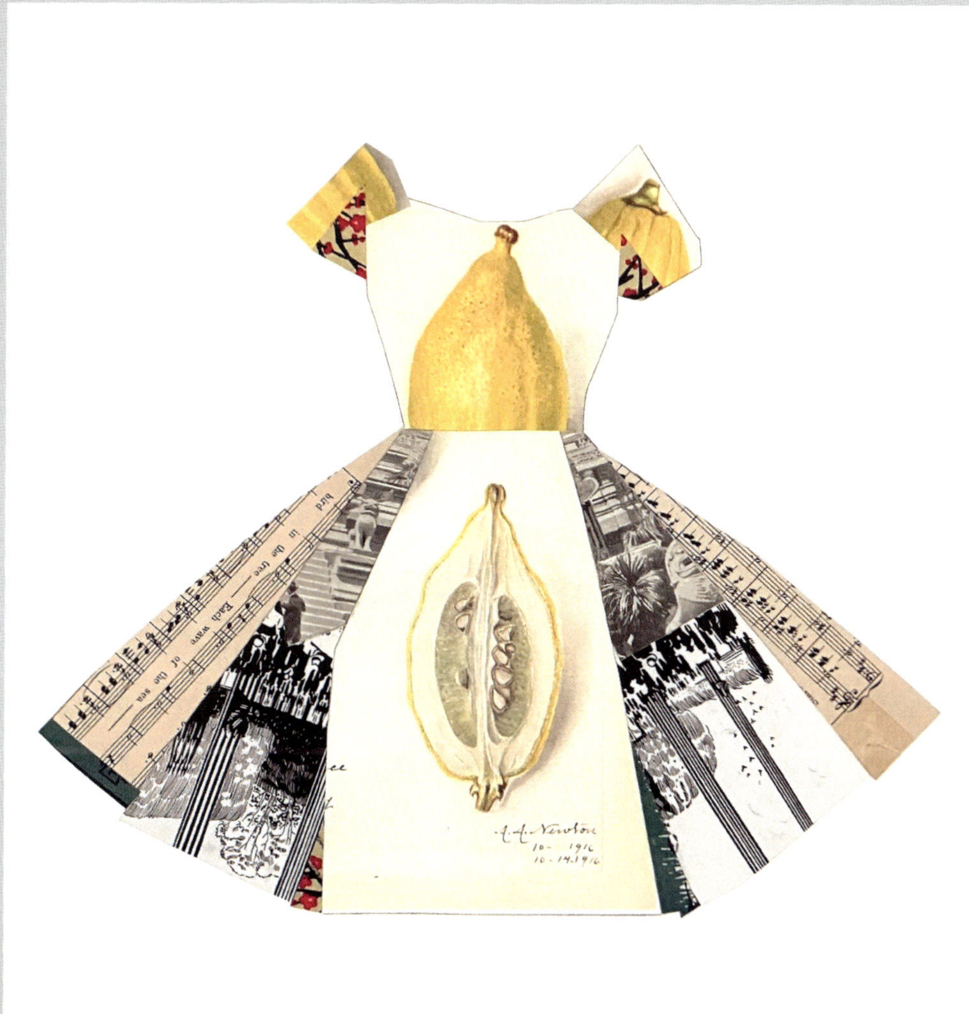
bird
in the tree
Each wave
of the sea

R

E

S

Crescent brooch—

bent to the shape

of the bark

I

N

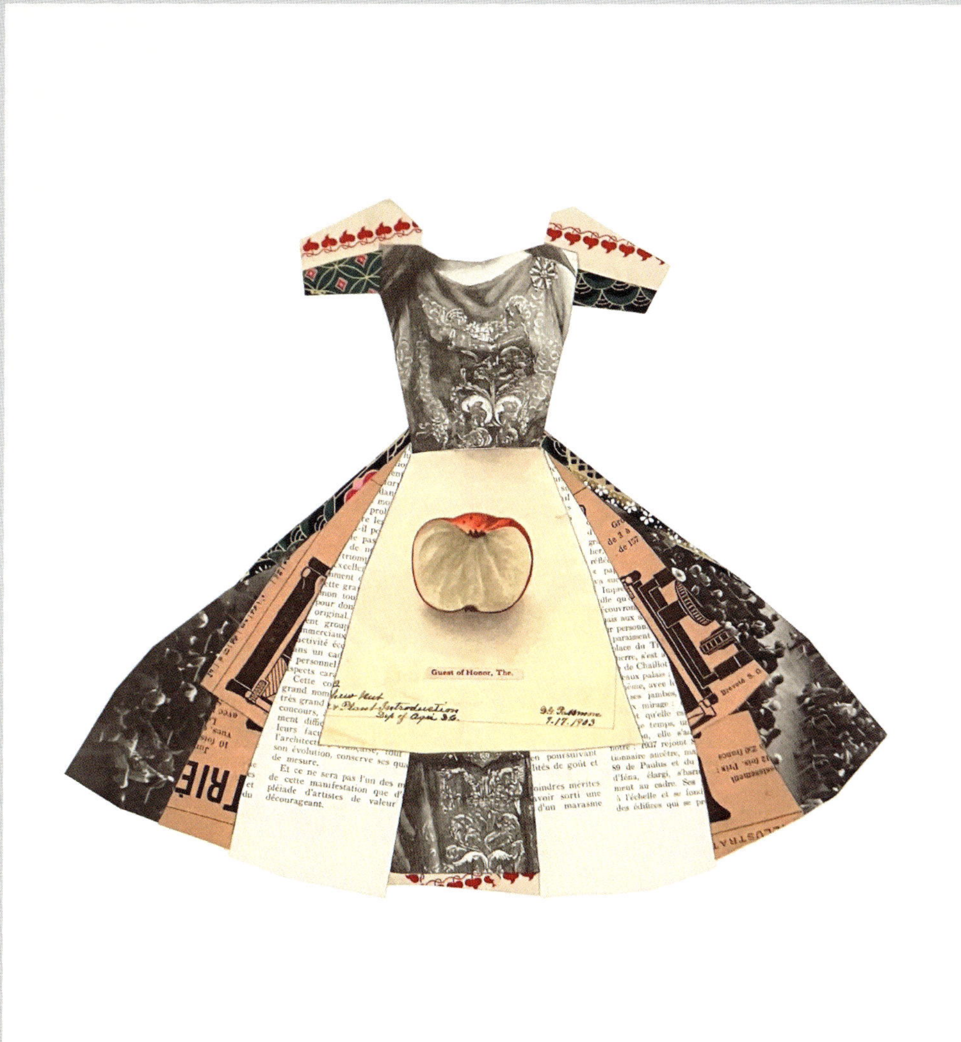
Guest of Honor, The.

C

L

The nightingale sings

to me to the mountain

to me to the mountain

D

O

U

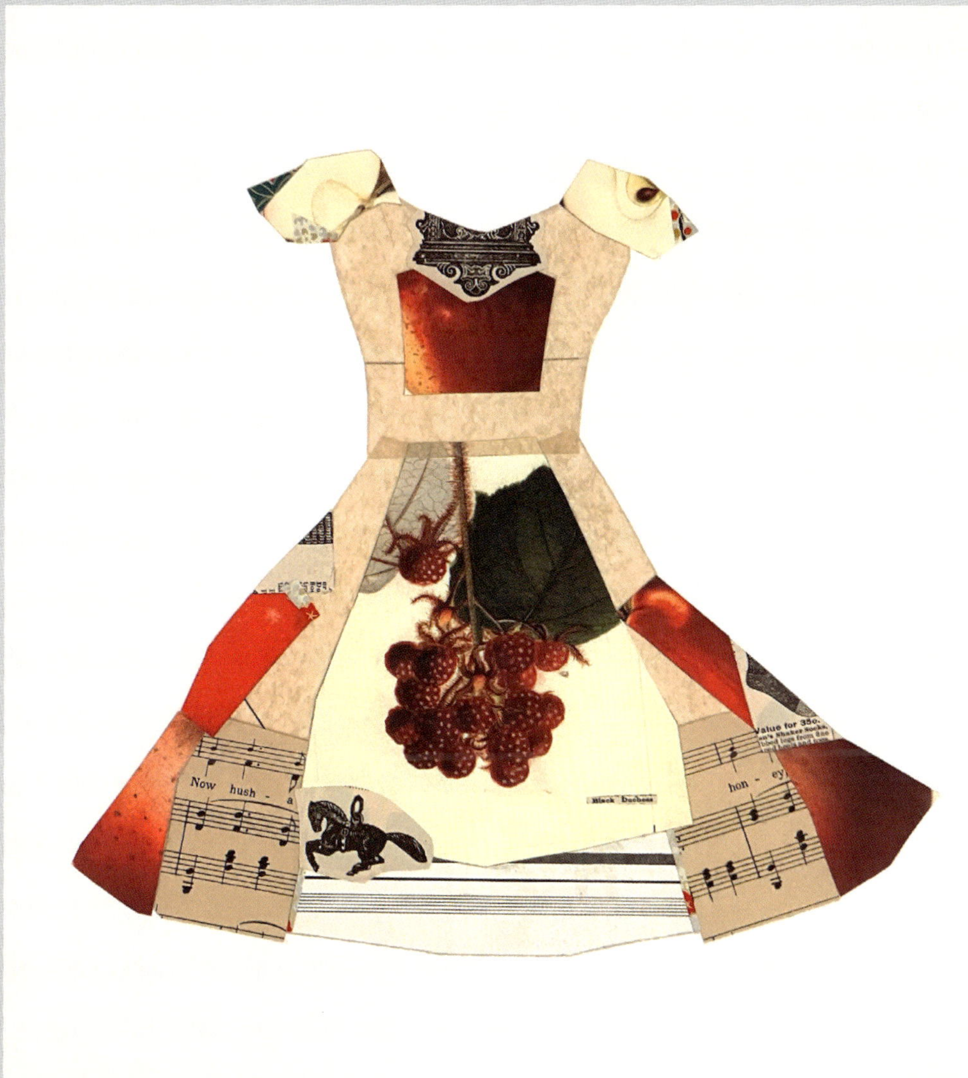
Now hush - a
Black Duchess
Value for 35c.
hon - ey

HUEWOODWHITE

HUE

A forest is a gift

Can you see me in this clearing?

I am no longer a woman

an imperative

Every drop has been stolen

The gone ice

the disappearing woods

We still see ourselves

as matter

Violet vanishes

forever

into the distance between what we have

what we have not done

and the bandages

We are savages

I bear a stain

        ash is not an endpoint

there are words that belong to it

but I can't say them

Dreams bury me

        what can be made dim

I am filthy

        can also be made bright

All day long

        each day is complete

I imagine myself as

        a circle

a bloom

        in a world that never notices

I carry time

a stone in a pail

impaled by starlight

an ache against my soul

my baroque beauty

diminishing

tamed by its occupation

Little feeder

soon the moon

crashes against my walls

the bones I refuse to forsake

will become visible

Overcast

iridescent

for ten thousand days

clouds

thirsty

in the middle of the night

shuffle

without a garden one is

twice

gray

If only it would snow

faraway

each heartbeat

thunder

echoes against the darkness

WOOD

I

who am the color of bark

all I was let go

I held out against his need

He swung me above his head

I stood beneath his rage

the known we were set free

I sang as the rage rained down

His scent thrills

sap is an open door

Once beloved

a moving drop

he cannot be wasted

one whorl

At night some trees

beyond price

release the unbearable

bait

A knot must be borne

despite its

unbearable

weight

Stripped

nowhere to go

no mere animal

mahogany

rootbound

he erases what he

inhales

Conflagration

thief of breath

burns everything

thief of will

to the ground

Ashes

I burst into flames

more and more

to forget

Smoke travels swiftly

infinite oxygen

shame

no path in sight

kills by degrees

tomorrow

arrested

green will end

memory

Rage leaves a scar

the flaw of living

wherever it touches

is love

the bridge between

the past and

my voice

present

and the window

opening

WHITE

Well water trembles

life makes meaning

as a splinter

out of the clouds

slips into

bulletproof

grief

Salt clears

evidence

I wait for tears

in the dark

beginning of March

we fall

one bespoke crocus

out of love

I cannot tell if I am lighter

with time

or if this haunting is the entire field

There is a bend to

loss

every soaked tree

hold on

unquelled desire

whole

wholly

the first time he brushed my nape

holy

I became a series of rooms

Still life

    intense cream

still alive

    the gardenia

For months I withheld my kiss

so he would crave my mouth

how it is not like his

how his could be a balm

possibly

or a bruise

this glistening emerges

The billions of worlds we form

not to be broken again

yet we cannot protect ourselves

from joy

The gone world

plastic globe

does not care

that I shake

what I never knew

the only place

I know

snow glows

un–Ruining

A sentence is a system

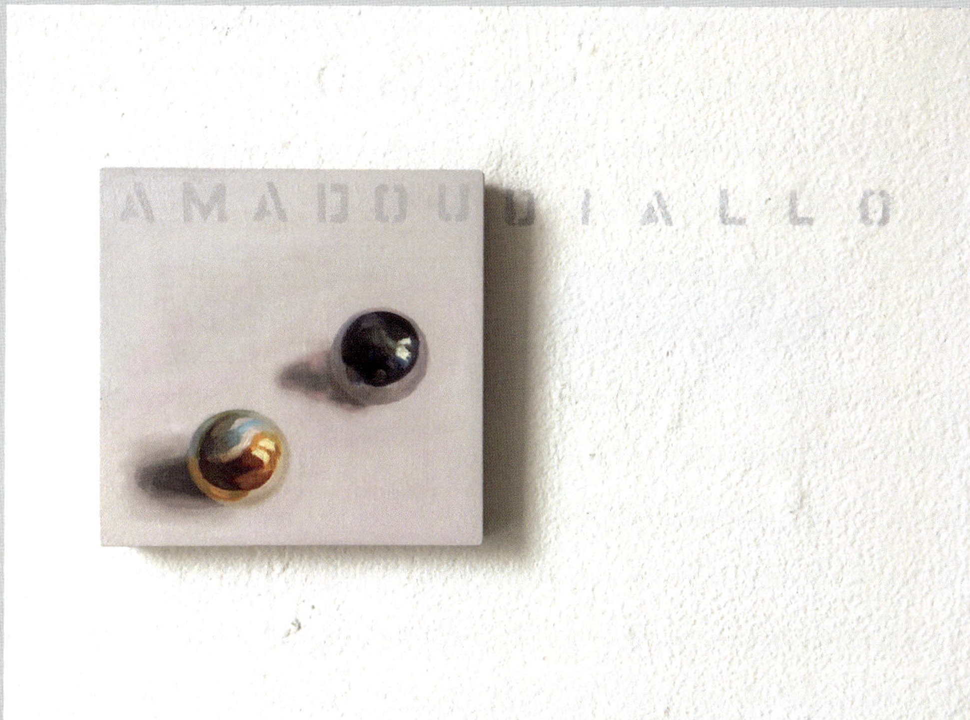
AMADOU DIALLO

sunlight outlines

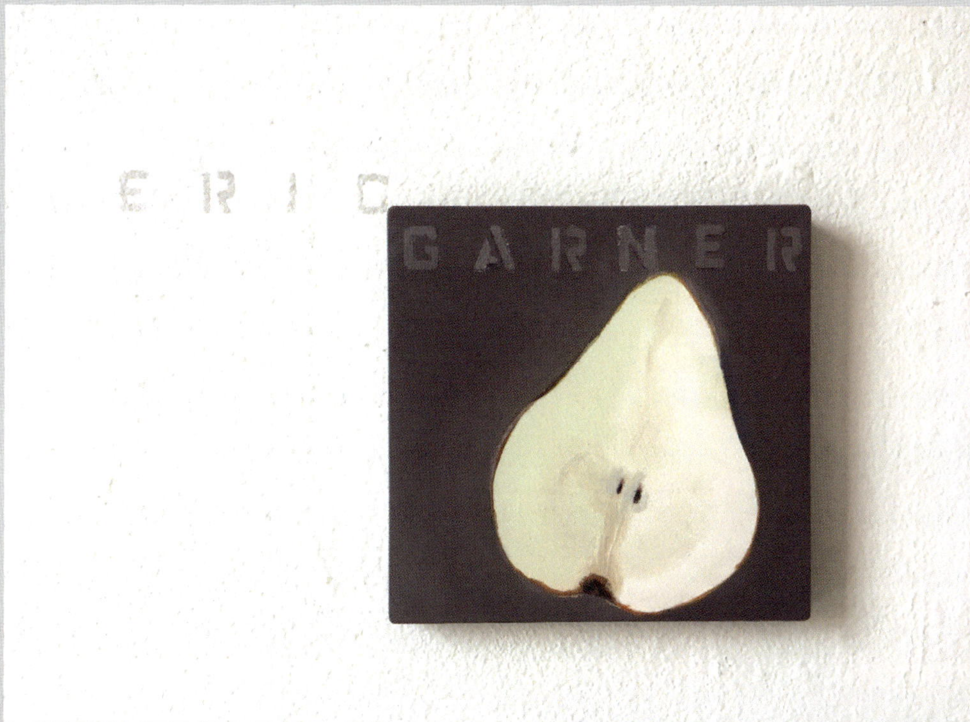
ERIC
GARNER

There is so much lightning in the body

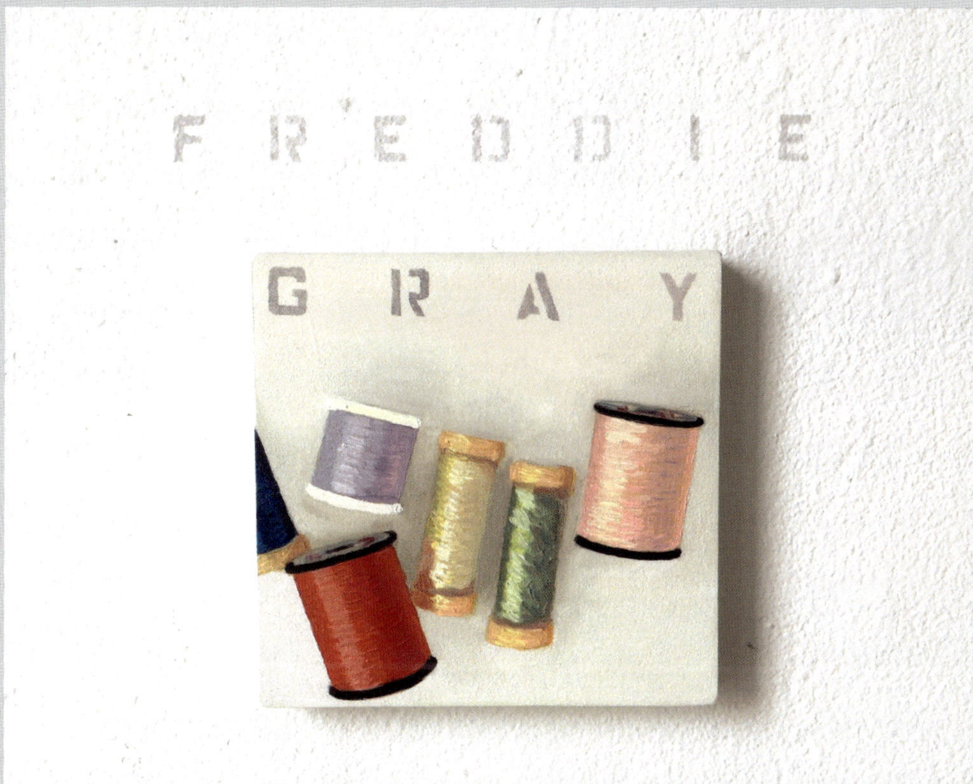
FREDDIE
GRAY

A cloud is a bribe

sometimes a fault

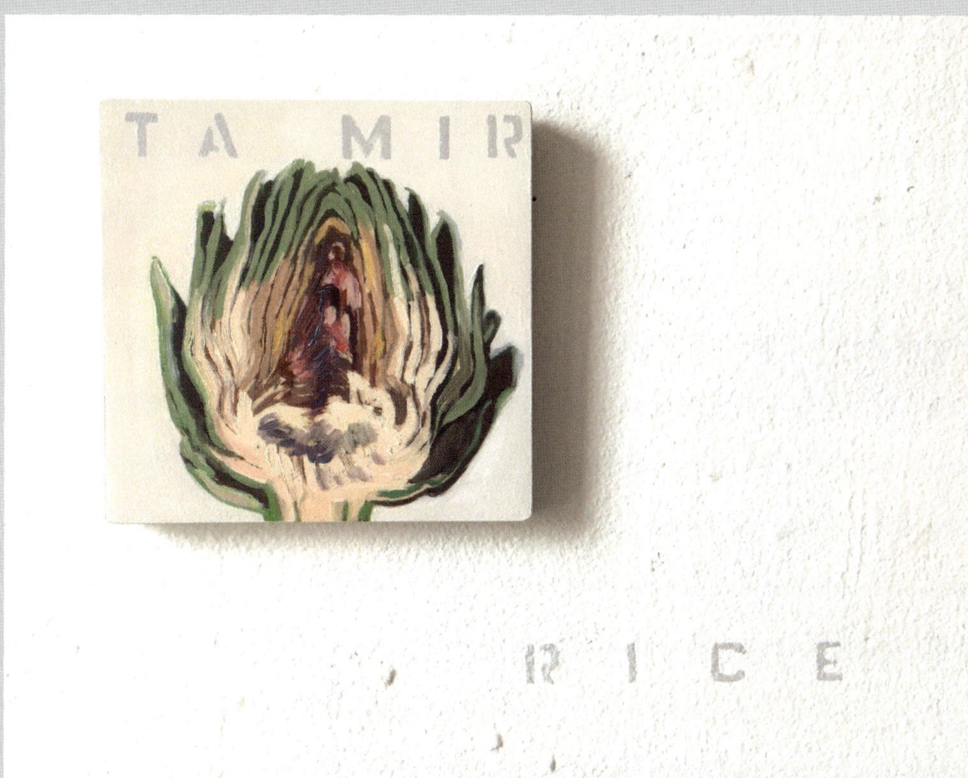
TA MIR
RICE

In this world everything rots

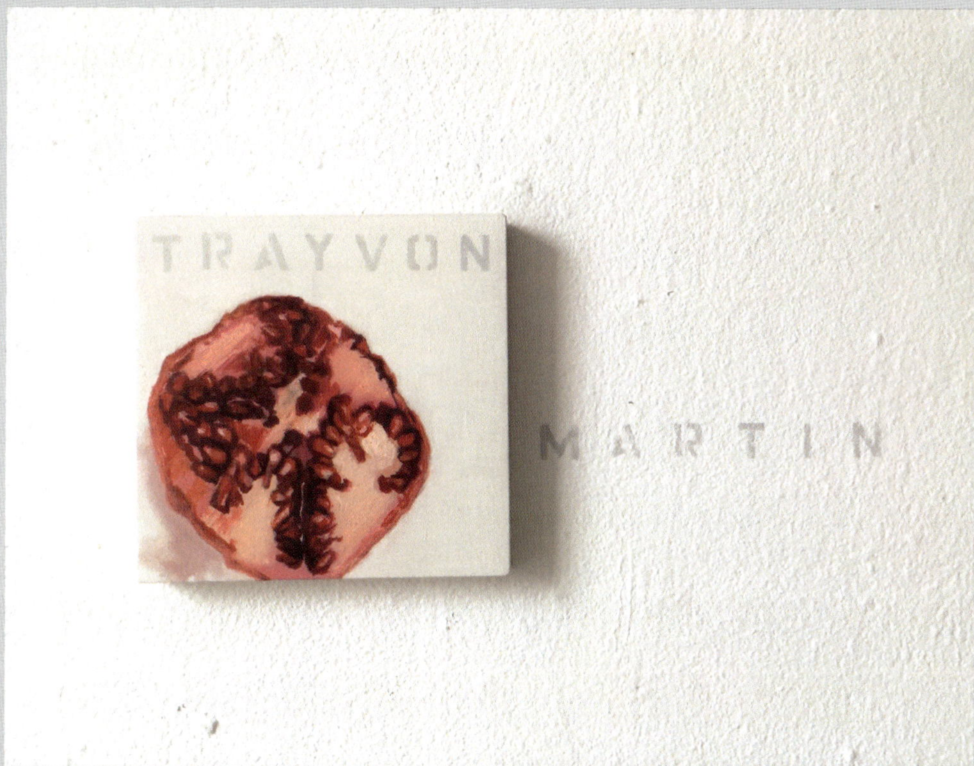
TRAYVON
MARTIN

When I clap

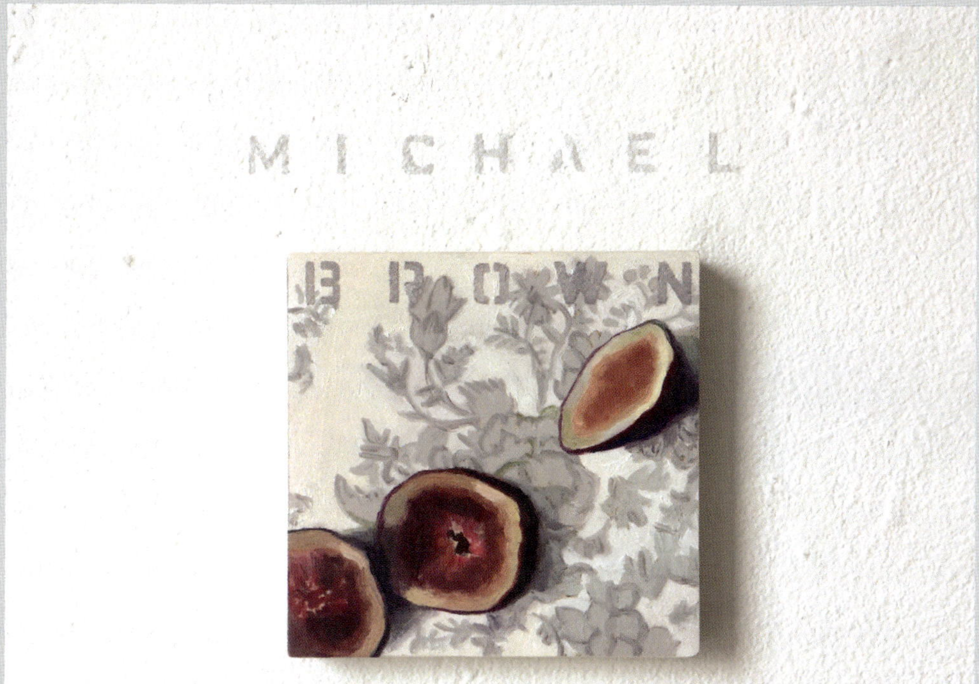
MICHAEL
BROWN

I can't stop

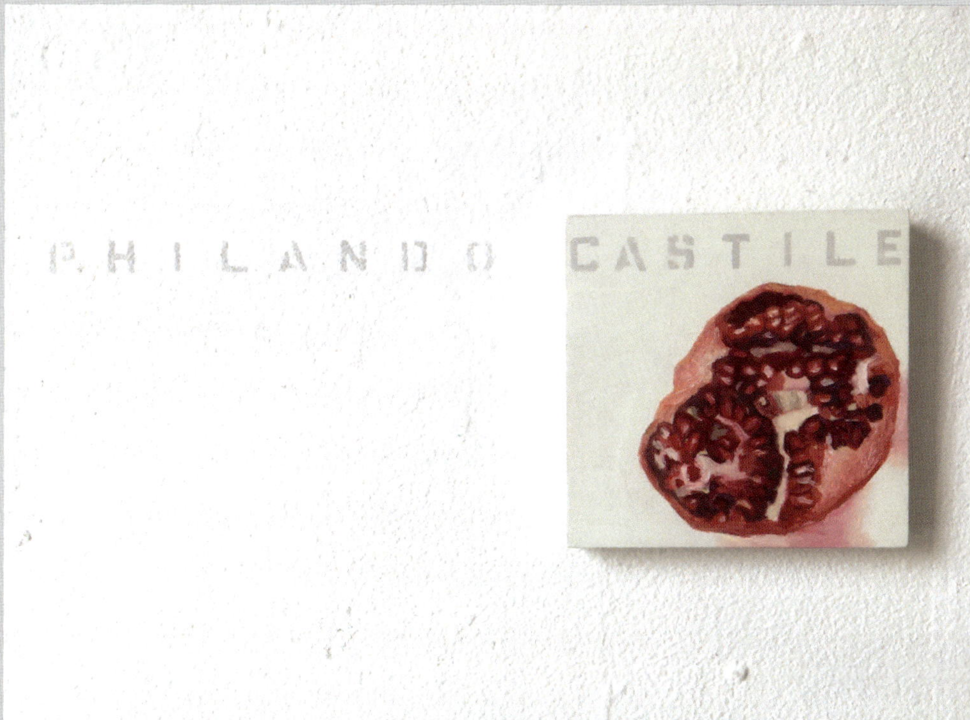
PHILANDO CASTILE

my lust for prisms

B L A N D

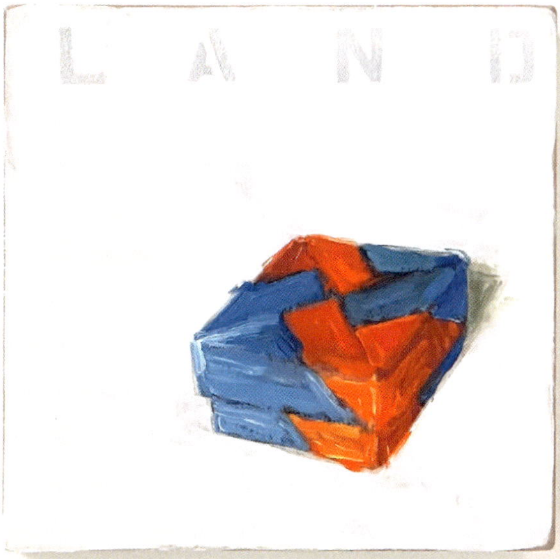

each hue

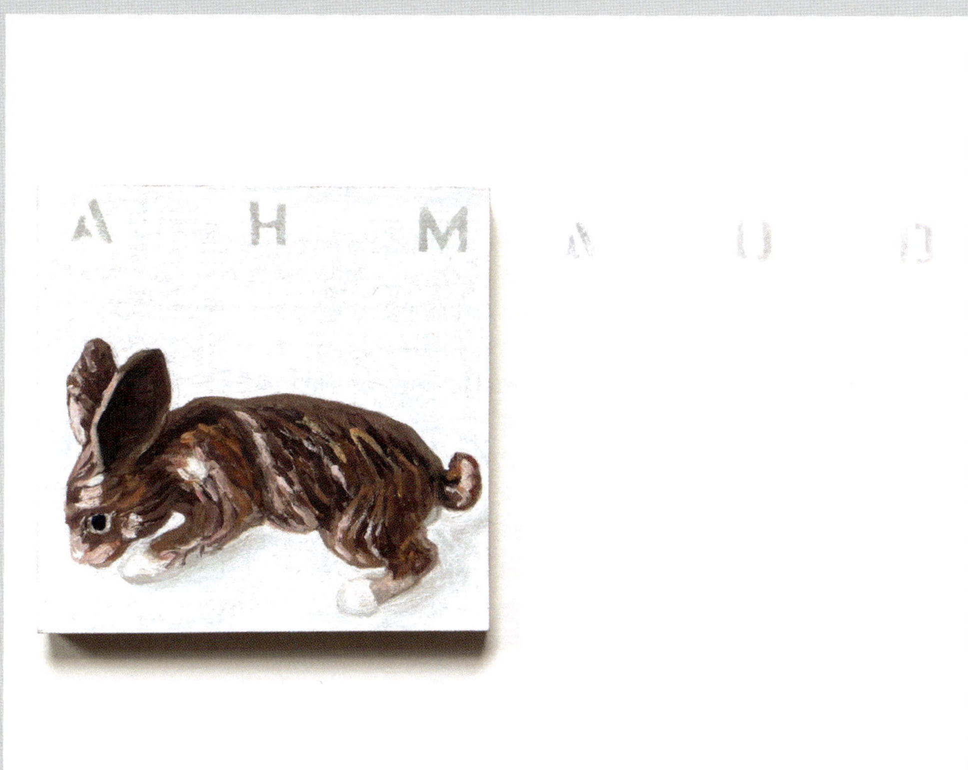
A H M A U D

a psalm

FLOYD

Notes

Excerpts in the section *Trigger Warning* come from: *A Domestic Cook Book: Containing a Careful Selection of Useful Receipts for the Kitchen*, self-published in 1866 by Malinda Russell, the first known cookbook published by a Black woman in the United States. The author's original spelling has been preserved in the recipe Queen's Party Cake: 'yelks' for yolks, in the recipe Cold 'Iceing' for Icing, and in Remarks: 'raise' for rise.

Special thanks to:

Katherine Leiner, Gretta Keene, Anne Adams, Mia Brandt, Marsha Grant, Gail Benjamin, and Lorna McFarland for always supporting my work, especially when it veers into new territories.

Elizabeth Murphy, editor-in-chief of Grid Books and Off the Grid Press, for her championship of my work and her belief in the magic of combining artistic disciplines.

Book designer Michael Russem for his expert eye and keen sense of harmony.

Gloria McFarland, Stephen Thomas, and Elisabeth Thomas for their love and support which are the centerpiece of my world.

Dillon Dyer for reading all of my news and cheering me on.

Schuyler Grant for lending his incomparable voice and heart to audio versions of my poems.

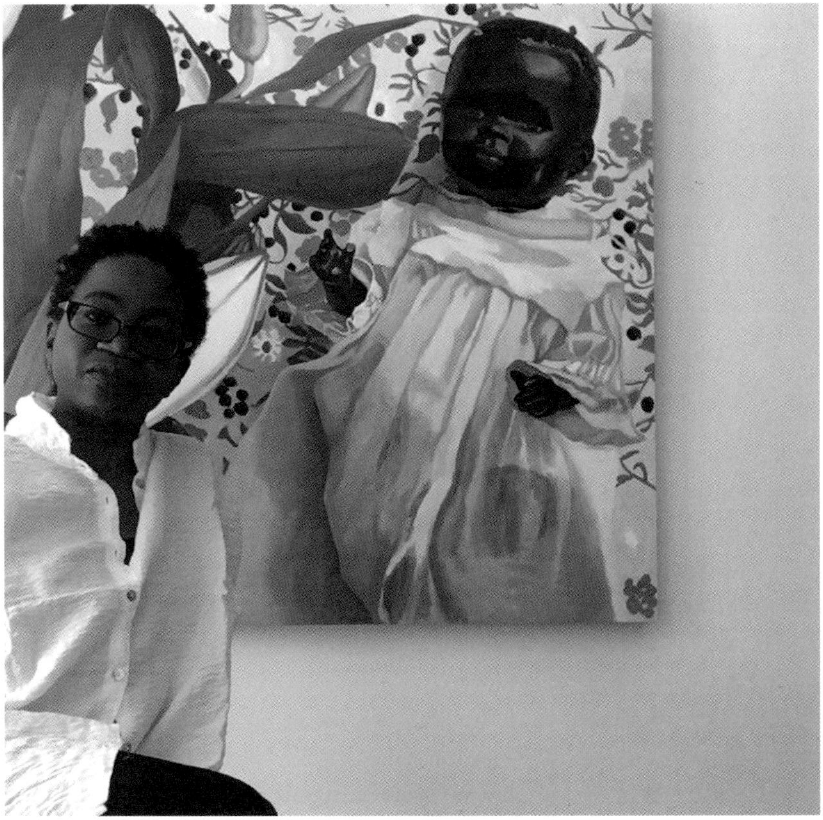

JoAnne McFarland is an artist, poet, and curator and the Artistic Director of Artpoetica Project Space in Gowanus, Brooklyn, which exhibits experimental and hybrid works that focus on the intersection of language and visual representation. JoAnne is the former Exhibitions Director of A.I.R. Gallery which was founded in 1972 as the first gallery in the United States specifically for women artists. She has artwork in the permanent collections of the Cooper Hewitt/Smithsonian, the Library of Congress, the Columbus Museum of Art, and the Department of State, among many others. JoAnne's poetry collections include: *Pullman*, *Tracks of My Tears*, *Identifying the Body*, *13 Ways of Looking at a Black Girl*, and *Acid Rain*. JoAnne has had fellowships at the Painting Center, the Bard Graduate Center Library, KALA Art Institute, the National Arts Club, the Van Alen Institute, and Cave Canem. Her recent exhibitions include *Affiliation* at the National Arts Club, *Queen For a Day* at the Bard Graduate Center Library, *Rights & Wrongs* at the Carroll Mansion in Baltimore, MD, and *Best & Brightest* and *The Indivisible Spectrum*, both at the Painting Center in NYC. JoAnne's artwork is represented by Accola Griefen Fine Art.